Thoughts After a Breakdown

Annika Edblom

BookLeaf Publishing

India | USA | UK

Presentation by *BookLeaf Publishing*

Web: www.bookleafpub.com

E-mail: info@bookleafpub.com

ISBN: 9789360949723

First edition 2024

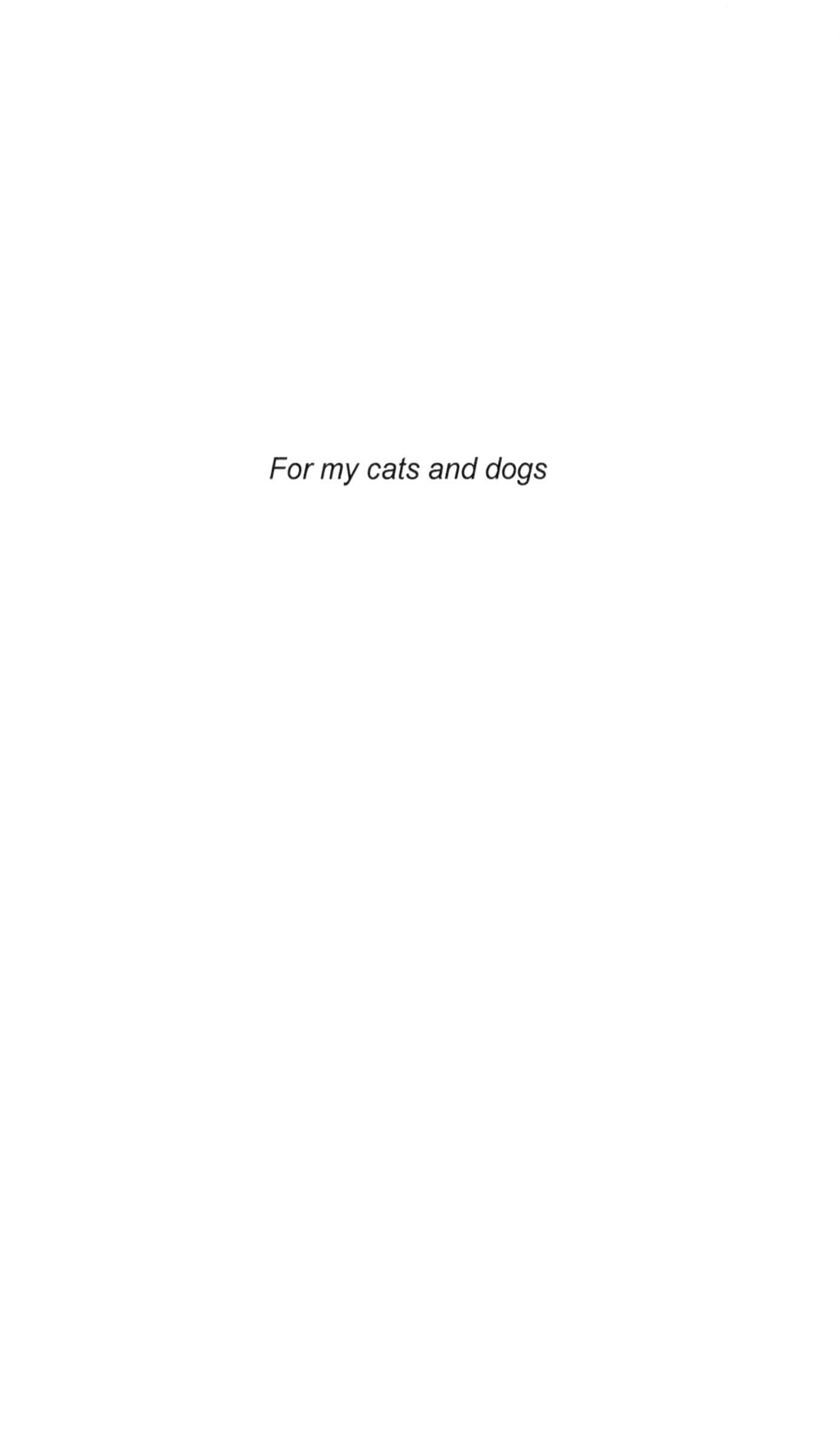

For my cats and dogs

Our Room

I've left the room
Where I used to hold our love, empty.
So sometimes I can go stand
In its vacantness
Layers of dust
Coating shelves, windowsills
Bare floors where our furniture
Used to live
I echo against the walls
Outlines where art
And memories used to hang
No one has lived here since
I like it that way.

Laundry Left in the Wash

If only I was broken
In a beautiful
Genius way.
Not the basic
All too familiar ways
Stereotypical in my bullshit.
If only I was insane
In a hauntingly inspiring way
A way that forged futures
Not dirty, mismatched socks.
Illuminating a path
Not littering it
With false starts and
Failed attempts.
Like all this nonsense should
Be for something wonderful.
But this isn't an endearing illness
Not enigmatic nor inspiring
Simply unwashed, unproductive
Madness smelling of dirty sheets and
Stale smoke
Missed appointments, unreturned calls
Just one more friendship like
The produce I picked out
With the best of intentions…

But forgot.
Left to rot
Well past its "best before" date
Maybe like me…
Best of intentions, spoiled
By moldy-smelling instability

Even a shell holds its shape
I am barely a husk
Hollowed out to the rind
Collapsing in concave shapes
Around the missing pillars of my life
Not even an echo can exist here
In the expansive, vacant chambers
Comprising my person
Where your love
Used to define me
Hallowed out like
Bird bones
Propped up with empty promises
And expectations.
"Fake it 'til you make it."

Make up a life of moments
Cigarettes
Loads of dirty laundry and
Fast food wrappers.
Watch my life go up
In smoke and empty bottles of
Detergent

You may have been
The one
To walk away
But I was
The one
Who let you

Both metaphorical and
Literal dead
Find home together
Inside my head.
These people
living through my
days and dreams
without ever being
present
but always here
if only they would leave.

Best Friend

8

We saw in each other everything
We despised about ourselves
And we loved each other
Fiercely for it

Refer to a person's feelings
When mentioning them to me
My memory is dependent
Upon revealing information
Oversharing is my appetizer
Boundaries have always been
A burden but
I. Am. Trying.
To grasp the concept
It's just difficult
To not put off anything
While simultaneously putting off everything
Oily, unwashed hair
The crown of clinical depression
No one will see me anyway
Not today anyways
And not tomorrow
I'm just going to get more
Food stains on this sweatshirt
I'm just going to sweat through my shirt
again tonight
While I battle the stress of sleep
It's too comfortable in my disaster

Let the crows have me
When I am finally done
With this body let it
Be of service at last
Finally providing sustenance
When I can finally be done
Lay me outside
call in a murder
So I can leave
My body for the crows

I let him peel it himself
Drops of sweet juice on the countertop,
He leaves behind the rinds
For me to clean up later
I let them sit
All dried up
Let them rot
All those "could've"s and "should've"s
I let him leave them
Mold doesn't grow on his mind
The way it grows on mine
Those dried-up peels
Will outlive us both

I never want to be a bird
I would be too cold
With the wind always
In my feathers
How would I sleep?
Terrified of toppling
Out of the nest, falling hard
down onto the ground

See?

13

If only you were thrilled to see
Whichever version of me
Showed up each day
In whichever way
If you loved everyone I am
Unconditional in your efforts
Free to be
Whoever I need

But what would I be
Without all my emotions
To boil me over

I haunt my house
Imprinting and ruminating
Sulking and simmering
Without a body
To keep me tethered

Selfies

If I don't take the photo
I'm sure I'll never remember
I'll forget every aspect of who I was
What I was called then and why
I've already lost so many of myselves
If I don't capture who I am
In this moment, in this photo
I'm sure I will lose myself
All over again

Feelings clawing
At the back of my throat
Stinging my eyes, choking
An allergic reaction
An Anaphylaxis of emotions
Set off with just
The hint of a breeze,
A hairpin trigger
And I'm engulfed
My heart in a vice
Crushing
Lost to the depth of it
All-consuming floods of feeling
Welling up from my chest
Pummeled by the waves of my
Self-created sea.

Soaked

18

My soul is tired
Sitting soaking wet
Heavy inside my body
I carry it like an anchor

All the places I left
Shards of myself
Here and there
Until I'm able to collect them
Whole once again

Name

This shirt smells like me
But I don't remember ever wearing it-
Or even seeing it before
Did I really pick this out?
Pick this up from somewhere?
Or was it gifted to me?
Did someone choose it carefully
Because they thought it would
Complement my complexion?
Or did someone select it
Because they liked it?
Is this something I've outgrown
Or did I always stretch, fold and rip
Trying to make it fit?
You can call me in whenever
To try on something new
But I'll need new measurements
They said at some point
I'd stop growing.

I started fires accidentally
Then on purpose.
Let the flames grow-
Unyielding
Rolling wild across my entire existence
Scorched earth
Until all that was left
Was me
My own fiery effigy.

A whole year I couldn't hear
Obscured with the sound of a cough
Four years fragmented
Jumbled together
Breaking, beaten
Against the unforgiving coast
Submerged disoriented
Blind and unknowing
Everything I struggle to shed
Forgetting everything I've let sink
Forever lost to the depths and dark
In my battle to breathe
To find the surface at last.

Breaking apart my dreams
Kindling for a fire
Snapping dry and brittle
Break the backbones of my hopes
Sacrificial acts
In the name of survival
Watch how they burn away
Warm myself a moment
Until their source is forgotten
Lost smoke, dissipating

Living years
Inside
Just a few days
Just a handful of hours
Mistakes made in minutes
Circling again and again
Again and again
Again and again
It all made sense
In the moment
Not now
Not any longer

I have no vision left
Where objects used to be clear
Now fuzzy, hazy, nondescript
I see no future here
Maybe I should make an appointment
With an optometrist

Now I'm afraid
Of owning more than I can carry
Afraid of caring
About more than I can drag behind me
So disheartened
Having to leave things behind
Homes I can never see again
I wonder who sleeps in my bed now

I'm careful now
To clip the wings
Of my expectations
Trying to temper
My dreams and desires
Refuse to let them
Grow with abandon
Too big for their pot

If everything I create
Can be toppled
Washed out and away
Blown asunder
Discarded to create
The debris for me
To stub my toe on
I see no purpose
In gathering them all again
The effort feels too futile.

Maybe I just want to be angry
Entitled to my rage
Justified in my fury
I will keep myself warm
With its embers
A hearth of hatred

I had almost conquered my mood
Until I started looking at photos
Mementos of memories
Now so bitter I choke
When just the hint of their taste
Touches my tongue

Stone cold in my chest
Where passion and purpose
Used to simmer and boil
Allowed to settle, stale
Congealed around my discarded dreams

My thoughts morphing
Slabs of cement and led
Laying down on my mind
Compressing, crushing
Gasping for air
Dry drowning in my depression
I've lost so much of myself
To dark days
More the same
Than the last
Strung together
Links in the chain
Keeping me bound to my bed

I'm sick of my own company
I want to tell myself
"It's getting pretty late.."
Lie and say I have an early engagement
I must not miss
Anything I can do or say
To get myself to leave at last

Will this one finally be the one?
The one pill to cure them all?
The exact chemical compound
To perfectly complement
My genetics'
Full potential
Darkness abated
Just 100 milligrams every morning

Trying to remember
Like trying to catch lit coals
Blisters and scars
Pieced together
Trying to form any explanation
Answers from the wounds

Engine overheating
Warning lights like-
Check oil!
Check oil!
Check oil!
Scorched, melting rubber
Just get through this intersection
Just get down this street
Just in time
Just before it kills
For good.
Done.
Check oil.
Check oil.
Check-

Am I anything any longer
But a burnt taste on their tongues
Left by their ruined expectations of me
I left the heat turned up too high
Never set the timer
Past the point of salvation
All anticipation for not
Left starving in disappointment
Lingering, stale
Smokey reminders of everything I did
And everything I did not become

I want to rip any version of me
From the memories and minds
Of everyone I've ever encountered
Claw every speck of me out
Of their brains
Left to wonder
What used to fill the bleeding gaps

A constant, always feeling
Resting heavy on my chest
Like I've forgotten something important
Something vital to my health and safety
Forgot I'm supposed to be running-
Fleeing from something
This unnamed threat
Breathing down my spine
My constant companion
I've never seen
Never lets me rest

If only I could
Put my phone down
Long enough to figure out
A purpose
Searching for meaning
In reaction videos and comment sections

Maybe in 30 years or more
I will drive up the hill
Brick house, middle of the block
Will be home to someone else
Different strangers
Living a different life
I wonder if they will let me-
If I even want to
See inside
Just for a moment
For the sake of remembering
I hope they can make a home of it
In all the ways
We never could

I can't get lost in my mind
anymore
I've set too many traps
Hidden too many landmines
not on purpose
but by circumstance
attempting to protect myself
the Winchester House
inside my brain

It's never been clear
Which parts of myself
I'm supposed to put on display
Which parts I'm supposed to pack away
I'm constantly redecorating
For the wrong holiday
Garland and tinsel
In August

My peace is precarious
Paralyzed in position
Sitting hiding in the eye
All my shame, swirling
An unrelenting whirling
Force for destruction
Sole purpose to
Suck me in
Thrash me around
Breaking my bones
Against all my transgressions
Unforgivable, unforgotten
Stranded in this
Vicious vortex

Instability
Like the most horrendous sunburn
The slightest touch
Unbearable, unimaginable
Excruciating paranoia

I am fractured
In ways and in places
I have no name for

I'm trying to see my thoughts
like leaves on a stream
But really they're leaves
gathered in a gutter
clogging and rotting

The processing system inside my brain
Feels unfamiliar
Like it switched to a software
I don't know how to use
I don't know how to open or close
anything

Since we stopped being friends
I have become that jar
Constantly expanding
In an attempt to hold all the grief
But the glass is stretching so thin
I'm waiting for it to shatter
With one heavy breath
I keep trying to empty it
Because this grief
Doesn't belong to me
I think I need to give it back
To people more deserving
How can I hold grief for your loss
When you were already lost to me?
I didn't know how
To extract only the toxic, codependent parts
While sparing all the love
A tumor
Coiled around my nervous system
There was no way to separate you
From me
Without damage

My breakdown tasted of acidity
The taste of corrosion and rust
Time sped up and slowed, simultaneously
Like the earth started spinning,
exponentially faster
But its rotation around the sun
Slowed to barely a crawl
All the while I was burning up and shivering
A fever of instability